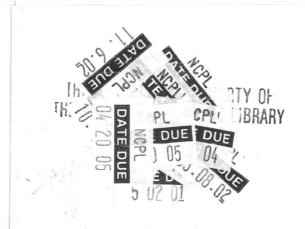

My First
REFERENCE LIBRARY

Our
BODIES

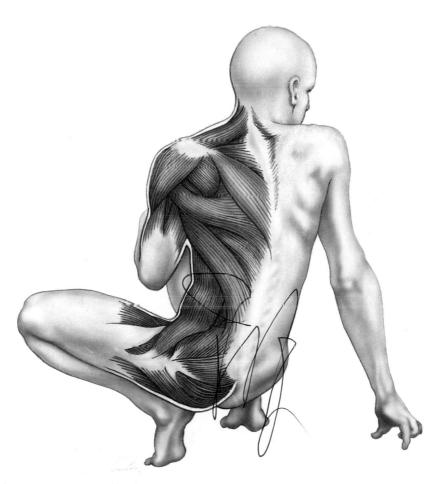

Adapted from Brian Ford's *The Human Body*

JULIE BROWN
ROBERT BROWN

Gareth Stevens Children's Books
MILWAUKEE

For a free color catalog describing Gareth Stevens' list of high-quality children's books, call 1-800-341-3569 (USA) or 1-800-461-9120 (Canada).

Library of Congress Cataloging-in-Publication Data

Brown, Robert, 1961-
    Our bodies / Robert Brown and Julie Brown.
        p.   cm. -- (My first reference library)
    Adaptation of: The human body / by Brian Ford.
    Includes bibliographical references and index.
    Summary: Describes the various parts of the human body and their functions.
    ISBN 0-8368-0080-X
    1. Human physiology--Juvenile literature.   [1. Body, Human.]
    I. Brown, Julie, 1962-   ,II. Ford, Brian J.   Human body. III. Title. IV. Series.
    QP37.B884   1990
    612--dc20   90-36755

North American edition first published in 1990 by
Gareth Stevens Children's Books
1555 North RiverCenter Drive, Suite 201
Milwaukee, Wisconsin 53212, USA

Photographic credits: Biophoto Associates, 10, 12, 15, 32, 37, 41 (bottom), 44; Colorsport, 47 (bottom), 53 (top); Steven Fuller 47 (top); Sally and Richard Greenhill, 13, 23, 50 (left); The Hutchinson Library, 5, 59: Camilla Jessel, 43, 51; Oxford Scientific Films, 52; Queen Victoria Hospital, East Grinstead, 53 (bottom); Science Photo Library, 7, 17, 29, 31, 39, 41 (top), 50 (right), 56; Spectrum Colour Library, 9, 35 (bottom); The Tate Gallery, London, 21; University College Hospital, London, School of Dentistry 55; John Watney, 19

Illustrated by Frank Kennard and Eugene Fleury

Cover illustration by Andrew DeWeert © 1990: The workings of the human body mystified scholars for centuries. Today, our understanding of this physical and mental marvel expands continually, leading to improved well-being.

Series editors: Neil Champion and Rita Reitci
Research editor: Jennifer Thelen
Educational consultant: Dr. Alistair Ross
Design: Groom and Pickerill
Cover design: Kate Kriege
Picture research and art editing: Ann Usborne
Specialist consultant: Dr. Margaret Rostron

Printed in the United States of America

1 2 3 4 5 6 7 8 9 96 95 94 93 92 91 90

Contents

1: THE HUMAN FORM

The Body

Humans start growing before they are born. Babies grow the fastest. By 18 years of age, most humans have nearly stopped growing. Not all parts of the body grow at the same rate. The head grows very little throughout life. Legs grow the most. ▼

Your body is flesh and bone, blood and water. It knows how to feed itself and how to keep the right amount of water inside. Your body knows how to escape from danger. Sometimes it acts faster than you can think. Your body can walk and talk. It can make friends and enemies. It has started to read this book. Your body can do many things that no computer could ever do.

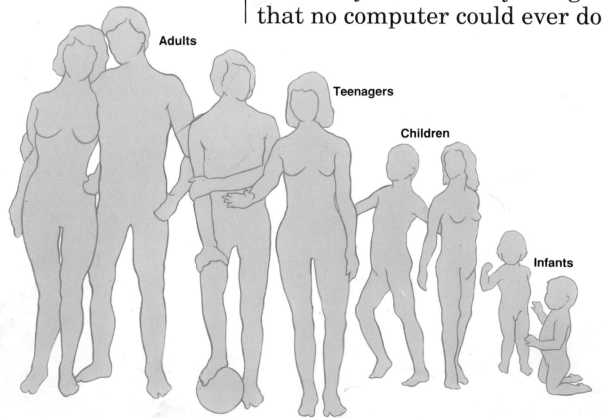

Adults

Teenagers

Children

Infants

Cells

Humans begin life as a cell in their mother's body. This first cell is very small, smaller than the dot over this *i*. Soon, the cell divides into two cells. As the cells keep dividing and growing, different types of cells begin to form. Some become skin cells, and others become cells of bone, blood, or muscles. Your body is a huge mass of cells — each one a tiny living thing. If every cell does its job right, you will be a healthy human being.

▲ The human species is called *Homo sapiens*. This Latin name means "wise man." Every human on Earth is a *Homo sapiens*.

As the baby grows inside the mother, the cells begin to form into special types for the work they have to do. These cells have different looks and sizes. Here are some examples. ▼

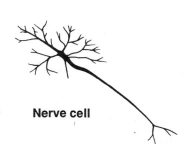

Nerve cell

White and red blood cells

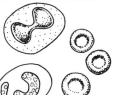

Muscle cells

Bone cells

The Skeleton

The skeleton gives the body strength. It gives muscles a place to attach, so you can move. Your bones also store calcium. If you don't eat enough calcium, your bones can become weak. ▶

Facts and Feats

• Each arm has 30 bones, and each leg has 29. Fourteen bones make up your face.

• You usually stop growing at age 18 (boys) or 16.5 (girls). After the age of 50, you will begin to slowly shrink.

• Bone is mostly made of two minerals — calcium and phosphorus.

• The human skeleton has the same number of bones as a horse's.

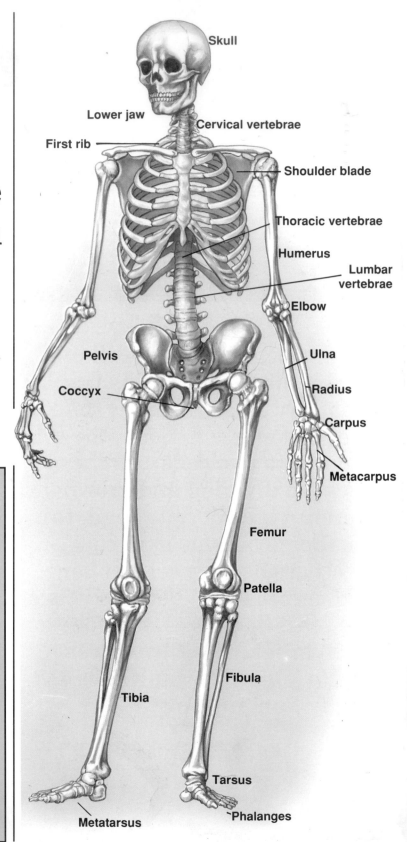

Skull

Lower jaw

Cervical vertebrae

First rib

Shoulder blade

Thoracic vertebrae

Humerus

Lumbar vertebrae

Elbow

Pelvis

Ulna

Coccyx

Radius

Carpus

Metacarpus

Femur

Patella

Fibula

Tibia

Tarsus

Metatarsus

Phalanges

A baby's body has over 300 bones. As the baby grows, some bones join together. Adults have only about 206 bones.

Types of Bone
- <u>Long bones:</u> These are the bones in your arms and legs.
- <u>Short bones:</u> The bones in your wrists and ankles are short.
- <u>Flat bones:</u> Flat bones, like the skull and pelvis, protect some parts of your body.
- <u>Irregular bones:</u> Inside your hands, feet, and ears are many bones with irregular shapes.

All bones have an inner bony network that looks like a sponge but is much harder.

The Spine
The spine is made up of 33 vertebrae. Each one is shaped like a spool. The spinal nerve cord runs down the center of the vertebrae, which protect it. Several brackets stick out from the vertebrae. Muscles join onto these. There are four kinds of vertebrae: cervical, thoracic, lumbar, and sacral.

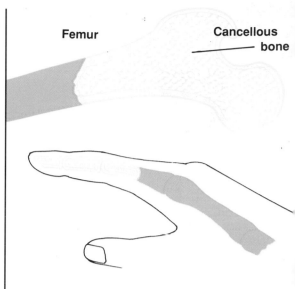

Femur
Cancellous bone

▲ The top of the thighbone, or femur, shows the strong bony network inside. This kind of inner bone makes red blood cells.

This x-ray shows irregular bones in a person's wrist. ▼

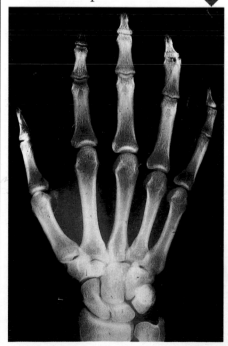

The Skull

This is a healthy skull, with strong bones and no signs of tooth fillings. ▶

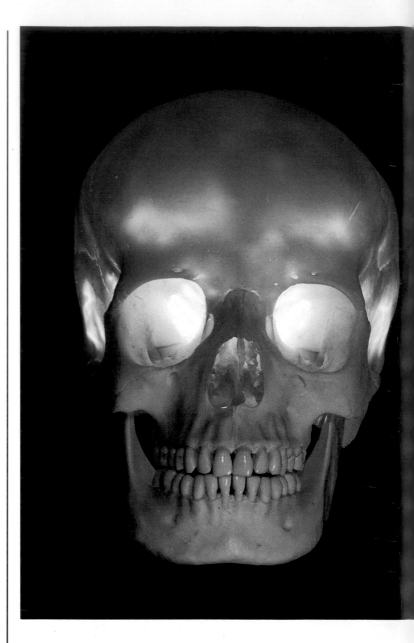

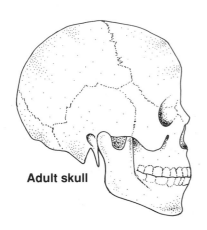

Adult skull

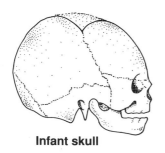

Infant skull

▲ The skulls of an infant and an adult are much the same. See how the teeth make the faces of the skulls look different.

The skull starts out as many flat, disk-shaped bones. These bones join together after you are born. The jaw is the only part of the skull that can move. Two rounded sockets hold the eyes. The delicate organs inside your ear are protected by the rounded sides of your skull. When all the soft tissues are removed, the skull looks like a smiling head with no eyes.

Parts of the Skull

Flat, thick bones make up the skull. Babies have a soft spot on top where four of the bones will grow together by the age of 18 months. Other flat bones make up the sides of the skull, the cheeks, and the jaws. An adult's skull shows wavy lines where the bones have joined. These are called sutures. Some air spaces inside the bones are called sinuses.

Since the time of the pirates hundreds of years ago, a skull and crossbones has meant danger. This symbol is still used as a warning sign on bottles of poison in some countries. ▼

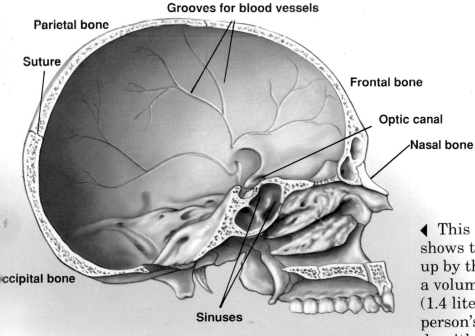

Grooves for blood vessels

Parietal bone

Suture

Frontal bone

Optic canal

Nasal bone

ccipital bone

Sinuses

◀ This section of a skull shows the large space taken up by the brain. Skulls have a volume of over 1.5 quarts (1.4 liters). The size of a person's brain has nothing to do with his or her intelligence.

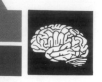

2: CENTERS OF LIFE

The Brain

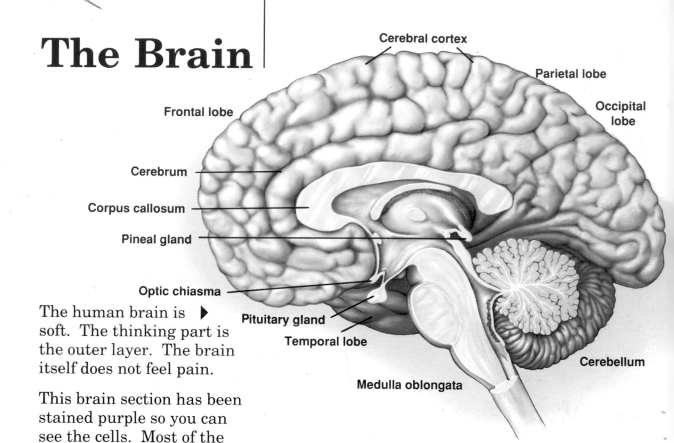

Cerebral cortex

Parietal lobe

Occipital lobe

Frontal lobe

Cerebrum

Corpus callosum

Pineal gland

Optic chiasma

Pituitary gland

Temporal lobe

Medulla oblongata

Cerebellum

The human brain is ▶ soft. The thinking part is the outer layer. The brain itself does not feel pain.

This brain section has been stained purple so you can see the cells. Most of the brain is made up of cell connections. ▼

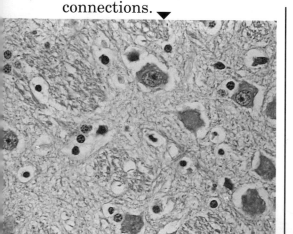

Brain Cells
There are about 15 billion cells in the human brain. Brain cells die off every day and are never replaced. But as you get older, you form more connections in your brain. Older people can think and work things out better than young people because older

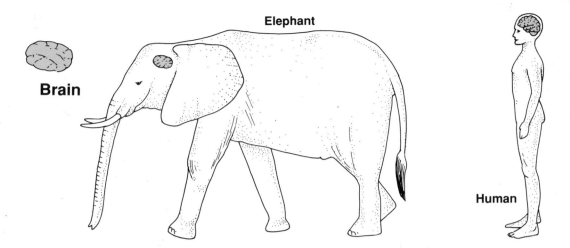

Elephant

Brain

Human

people have more connections among their brain cells.

Areas of the Brain

The cerebellum, located at the back of the skull, controls your coordination. The frontal lobes, in the front of your brain, have areas that make you move and behave as you do. Other areas control seeing, hearing, and touch. Intelligence lies in the cerebral cortex — the outer layer of the brain. The human brain is so big that it has to be folded up to fit inside the skull. The nerves that enter the skull cross over, so that the left half of the brain controls the right half of the body, and the right half of the brain controls the left half of a person's body.

▲ Some animals have larger brains than humans. Although elephants have bigger brains than humans, people are more intelligent than elephants.

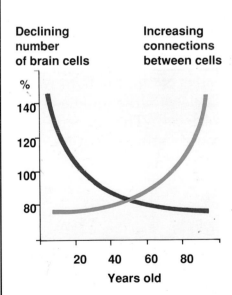

Declining number of brain cells

Increasing connections between cells

▲ The red line shows how many brain cells you have left as you age. The blue line shows the growing number of cell connections you make as you age.

The Nerves

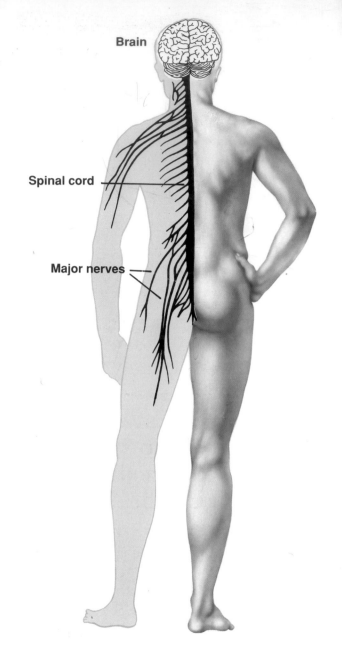

Brain

Spinal cord

Major nerves

The brain connects to the ▶ rest of the body through the spinal cord. Damage to the spinal cord by injury or disease is serious because it stops the nerve signals from getting through.

A brown stain has been used to show these nerve cells. Notice the light round nucleus in the middle of each cell. This nucleus controls the cell's work. ▼

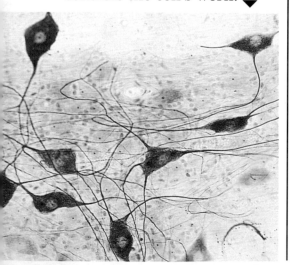

Long, thin nerve cords run all through your body. They carry signals from one part of the body to another. The ends of these nerve cell branches lie very close together, but they really do not touch each other. A small gap called a synapse lies between the ends. The nerve signals

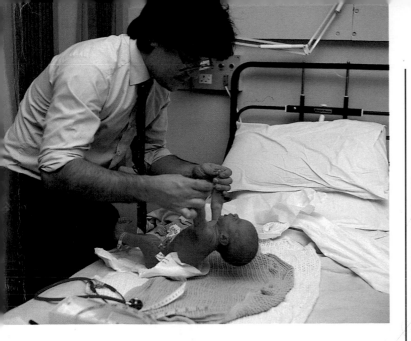

◀ Many actions — like a baby's holding onto a doctor's fingers — are reflexes. They work without you thinking about them.

Did You Know?

• Nerve signals can travel at a speed of 370 feet (113 m) per second.

• A person's brain has billions of nerve cells. An ant's brain has only about 250.

• From the spinal cord, 31 pairs of nerves go out to the rest of the body.

pass chemically across this synapse, going from cell to cell.

Reflexes

Many nerves go directly to the brain so that you can tell what is going on in your body. But others go from one set of nerves to another. These nerves control your reflexes — actions that your conscious mind does not control. Sneezing is a reflex reaction; you cannot decide to sneeze.

The Spinal Cord

Most nerves join together to form the spinal cord, which runs through your backbone. If this main nerve cord is injured, your body will not work properly below the damaged area.

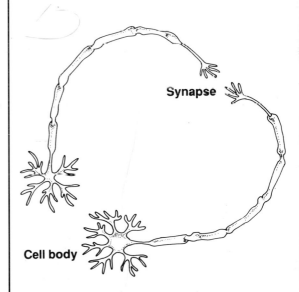

▲ Nerve cells send out many branches to gather information. But only one long branch, called the axon, sends signals.

The Liver

The liver is the largest organ in your body. It weighs about three pounds (1.4 kg) and is brown-red in color. It stretches right across the body and is up to six inches (15 cm) thick. The lower part of your ribs protects the liver.

The Living Organ

The liver produces and stores energy from the food you eat. Blood coming from the liver is always warm — it helps heat your body. The liver breaks down harmful things in your blood, such as bacteria, drugs, and toxins, or poisons. Your liver also makes vitamin A from

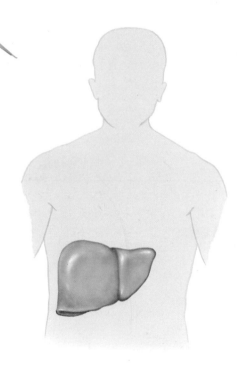

▲ The liver lies across your body, just inside the lower part of your ribs.

Right under your liver is a ▶ green bag called the gall-bladder. It contains bile, which helps you digest fats and oils.

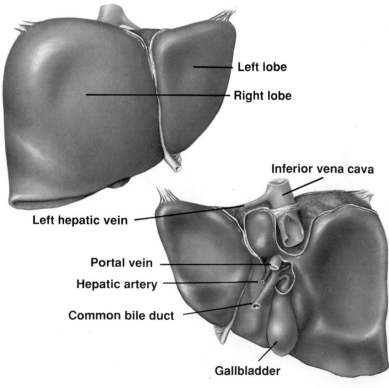

Left lobe

Right lobe

Inferior vena cava

Left hepatic vein

Portal vein

Hepatic artery

Common bile duct

Gallbladder

carotene, which is found in vegetables such as carrots. The liver makes bile, a fluid that helps digest fats. Drugs, alcohol abuse, and virus infections and other diseases can damage the liver. This is serious because the liver is needed for life.

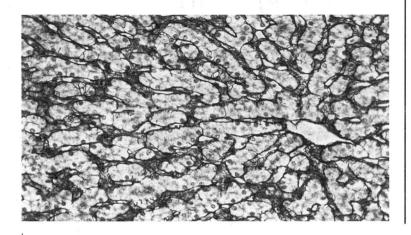

A purple stain has been used so you can see how liver cells form channels. Blood flows through these spaces, collecting useful materials and getting rid of wastes. The liver does not have vessels for this blood flow. But bile, made by the liver, goes through ducts, or tubes, ◀ to the gallbladder.

This drawing shows how the blood moves inside the liver. This picture is much simpler than the liver in real life. ▼

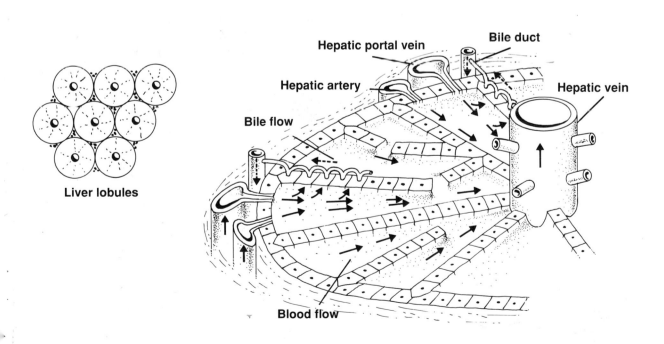

Liver lobules

Hepatic portal vein

Bile duct

Hepatic artery

Hepatic vein

Bile flow

Blood flow

The Blood System

Blood moves out from the ▶ heart to go around the body through arteries (red). The blood returns to the heart through veins (blue). There are, of course, veins and arteries on both sides of the body.

Did You Know?

• People once thought that some illnesses were caused by too much blood. Doctors used leeches to suck out the "extra" blood.

• People living in high places, with thinner air, have more red blood cells. These carry less oxygen.

• Over half your blood is a liquid called plasma. The rest is made of cells. The plasma is mostly water.

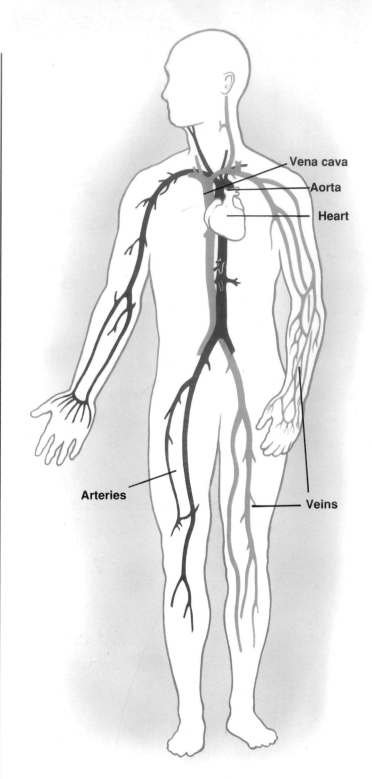

Vena cava

Aorta

Heart

Arteries

Veins

Red Blood Cells

Blood is a liquid tissue that takes oxygen and food to the body's cells and collects their

◀ Red blood cells (left) are the only cells in the human body without a nucleus. The place where it was leaves a dent in the middle of the cell (below). White blood cells are colorless and have different shapes. Platelets are pieces of cells that help you stop bleeding. ▼

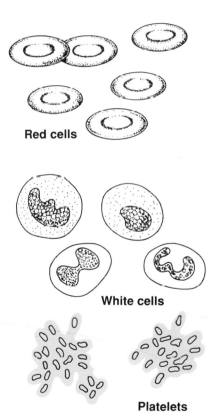

Red cells

White cells

Platelets

wastes. An adult human body has about six quarts (5.7 liters) of blood. Over half of this is fluid, and nearly all of the fluid is water. Blood has red cells and white cells. Most of a red cell is hemoglobin, a material that turns red when it meets oxygen. Hemoglobin picks up oxygen when the blood passes through the lungs. Each red blood cell lives for about four months and then dies. New red blood cells form in the marrow of bones.

White Blood Cells

There is only one white blood cell for about every 600 red blood cells. The white blood cells help control infections by destroying microbes. Tiny platelets help stop the bleeding if you get cut.

The Lungs

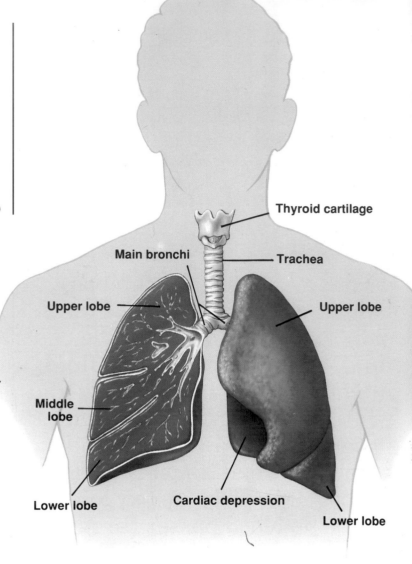

Thyroid cartilage

Main bronchi

Trachea

Upper lobe

Upper lobe

Middle lobe

Cardiac depression

Lower lobe

Lower lobe

This drawing shows what ▶ the lungs look like. The one on the right is whole. The one on the left has been cut through to show what is inside. The lungs fit tightly under the ribs, with hardly any space left over. In the lung on the right, you can see a large dent — the cardiac depression. This is where the heart fits.

The lungs are like soft, moist, delicate sponges. In the lungs, air comes together with blood. The windpipe, or trachea, leads down to the lungs. There, it divides into tubes called bronchi, and then into smaller and smaller tubes that end in thin tissue bubbles, called alveoli. Each alveolus is filled with air and is covered with tiny blood vessels, called capillaries. These blood vessels are so thin that blood cells have to squeeze through one at a time. The red cells pick up fresh oxygen from the alveolus and give it the waste carbon dioxide that they carry.

Breathing

Your lungs can hold about five or six quarts (5-6 liters) of air. But when you breathe, you usually take in (and let out) only about one-tenth of this. Most of the air stays inside to keep the lungs inflated so they will work. Lungs can be harmed by air pollution and smoking.

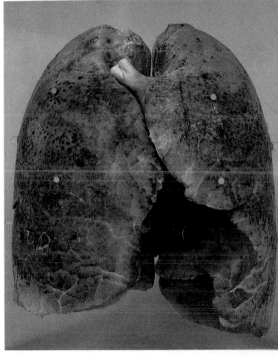

These are actual human lungs. Lungs are not normally this dark color. These diseased lungs came from a heavy smoker. ▼

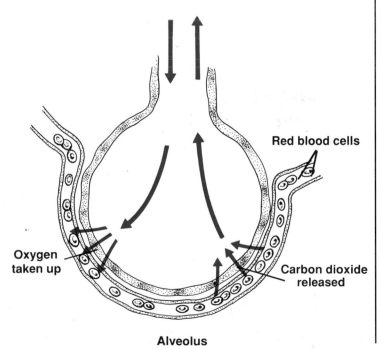

Red blood cells

Oxygen taken up

Carbon dioxide released

Alveolus

◀ The airways in the lungs get smaller and smaller until they form tiny, round, spongy bubbles called alveoli. This drawing shows a single alveolus. Around it move the red blood cells in their capillaries, collecting oxygen and giving up waste carbon dioxide.

Seeing

Optic nerves connect the eyes to the brain, which helps the eyes see. Specially arranged muscles help keep the eyes in their sockets and let them turn in many directions. ▼

Inside the Eye

The human eye is 1,000 times more sensitive than the best photographic film. In front, a tough layer, called the cornea, protects it. Behind this is the pupil, an opening that lets in light. Around this is the iris, the colored part of the eye that can make the pupil bigger or smaller

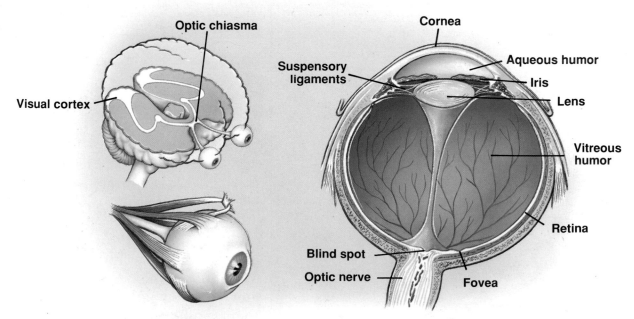

Optic chiasma

Cornea

Visual cortex

Suspensory ligaments

Aqueous humor

Iris

Lens

Vitreous humor

Retina

Blind spot

Optic nerve

Fovea

Right eyeball and muscle

to let in more or less light. The lens, behind the iris, focuses by getting thinner or thicker. Behind the lens, the eyeball is filled with a clear fluid called the vitreous humor. Light rays shine in through this fluid and make a pattern on the retina — the inside lining of the eye. The retina has special cells: cones, which see color, and rods, which see only black and white.

Seeing and the Brain

The retina sees an upside-down image of what we are looking at. The brain's job is to turn the image around so that everything looks right side up. The eyes and brain work together to help us recognize what we see.

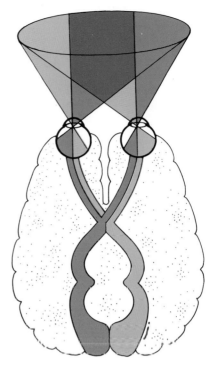

▲ This drawing shows how the brain blends a flat view from each eye to make one 3-D picture.

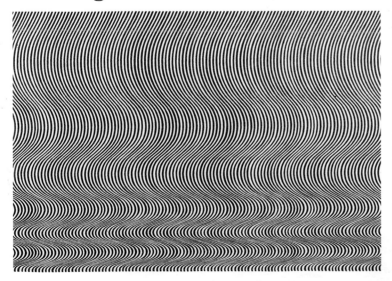

Facts and Feats

• Bees cannot see red. Sharks see only grays.

• Eight out of every 100 men are color-blind — they can't see some colors.

• Ancient Egyptians used raw animal livers to cure night blindness.

◀ If you stare at this picture long enough, it will seem to be moving because your brain needs to sort out all the details.

Hearing

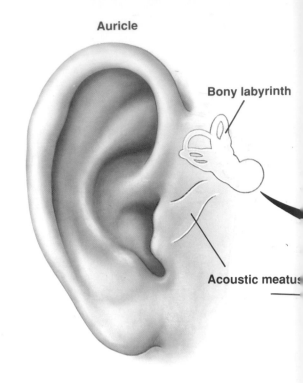

Auricle

Bony labyrinth

Acoustic meatus

Facts and Feats

• Many mammals, such as bats and dogs, can hear sounds of a much higher pitch than humans can hear.

• Even with your eyes shut, you can tell almost exactly where sounds are coming from.

• Crickets can hear with their legs! They have special membranes there that act like eardrums, over air chambers with nerve fibers inside.

We usually think of an ear as something outside of the head. But that is only the outer part of the ear. It collects the sounds and sends them down into the ear canal. Inside this canal are the eardrum and three tiny bones.

How We Hear

Sounds hit the eardrum and make it shiver, or vibrate. The eardrum, in turn, makes the tiny bones — called ossicles — vibrate. The ossicles pass the vibrations on to the cochlea, which is shaped like a snail's shell and filled with fluid. Inside the cochlea lies the organ of

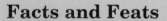

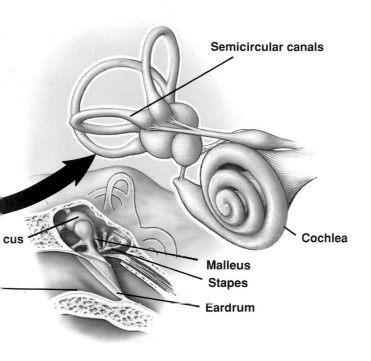

Semicircular canals

cus

Malleus

Stapes

Eardrum

Cochlea

◀ The outer ear collects sounds and sends them down the ear canal to the eardrum. The arrow points to a larger drawing of the inner ear. The three ossicles are the malleus (hammer), the incus (anvil), and the stapes (stirrup).

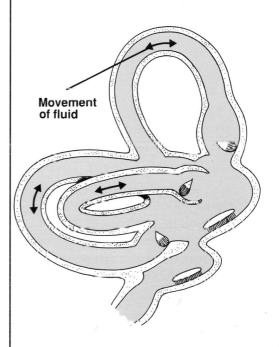

Movement of fluid

Corti, which has 20,000 tiny nerve fibers. When the sound vibrations make waves in the cochlea's fluid, this makes the tiny nerves send signals to your brain, so your brain can tell you what sound you are hearing. Very loud noises, such as air hammers or loud music, can damage the organ of Corti.

▲ When you move your head, liquid moves in three curved structures, called the semicircular canals, in the inner ear. Tiny sensors there track your motion to help you keep your balance. If you spin around and then stop suddenly, the fluid keeps sending signals to your brain, and this makes you dizzy.

◀ This Chinese acrobat is an expert at balancing.

Smell and Taste

Your sense of smell begins ▶ in a brown-colored area deep inside your nose. It is a very powerful sense that could save your life or bring memories from long ago. Your sense of smell is 10,000 times stronger than your sense of taste.

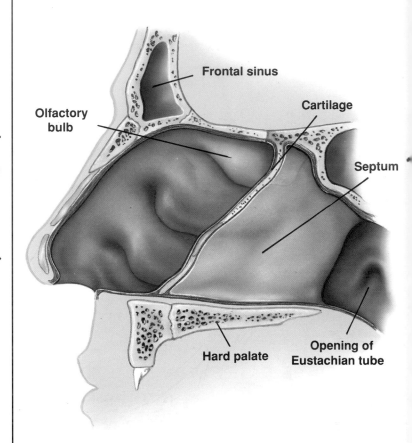

Frontal sinus

Cartilage

Olfactory bulb

Septum

Hard palate

Opening of Eustachian tube

Seven Kinds of Odors

1. **Ethereal** — fruity
2. **Camphorlike** — like mothballs
3. **Musky** — musklike
4. **Floral** — flowerlike
5. **Minty** —mintlike
6. **Pungent** — vinegary
7. **Putrid** — like rotting food

Your sense of smell gets tired easily, so you "get used to" a certain odor.

Your nose warms up air before it goes to the lungs, keeps out dust and bacteria, and tells odors with the olfactory bulbs high up inside the nose. The bulbs have cells with very tiny "hairs." Odors trigger these hairs to send messages to the brain. An odor is made up of tiny particles that you breathe in with the air. The kind of odor depends on the shape that the particle has.

24

Good, Bad, and Ugh

Your sense of taste is closely linked to your sense of smell. Some people think rotten fish smells bad, but the Inuit people of the Arctic think it smells great because it tastes so good. You taste things when foods or liquids touch different taste buds on your tongue. The taste buds send different messages to your brain. The tongue has separate areas that taste sweet, sour, salt, and bitter.

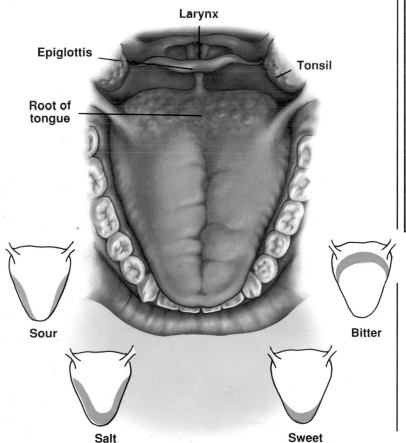

Larynx

Epiglottis

Tonsil

Root of tongue

Sour

Bitter

Salt

Sweet

A Trick of Smell

Animals identify by smell. Shepherds can trick a sheep that has lost its lamb into feeding an orphaned lamb. The shepherd skins the dead lamb and ties the skin over the orphan. The mother sheep smells the odor of her dead young and thinks the orphan is her own. Soon the mother gets used to the new lamb's real odor.

A Trick of Taste

Two plants can change the way you taste sweetness. In India, chewing the leaves of one plant keeps you from tasting any sweetness for a time. In West Africa, the miracle berry makes sour food taste sweet for hours. Africans who chew one of these berries find that sour bread and sour palm wine will taste sweet. So will lemons!

◀ Your tongue is covered with little sense organs called taste buds. Each area of the tongue can taste a different flavor.

25

The Skin and Touch

Facts and Feats

• The Chinese found out how to use fingerprints for identification 1,300 years ago.

• Your fingerprint may contain an arch, a loop, a whorl, or a blend of all three shapes.

The skin is the largest organ of the human body. Many nerves in the skin help us know that the things we touch are hot or cold, rough or smooth, soft or hard. Skin keeps microbes from entering our bodies and shields us from the Sun's rays.

Temperature Control

Our skin controls our body's temperature. When you walk or run, your muscles release heat. When your blood becomes too warm, your skin's blood vessels get bigger to release this heat and help cool you down. Your skin also helps cool you with

Your bedroom may have ▶ thousands of microscopic creatures like this one. They are dust mites that eat the dead skin cells that flake off your body.

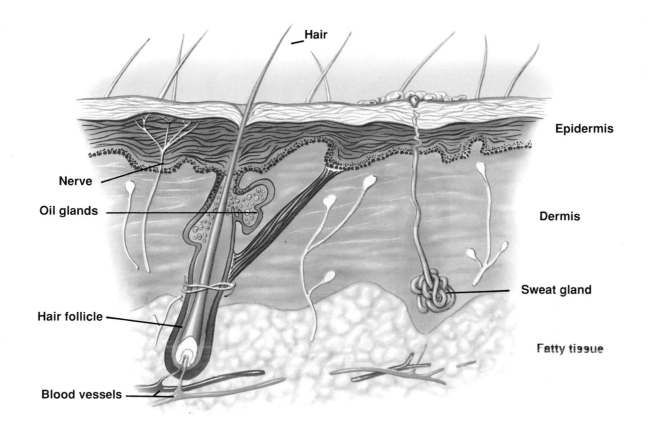

Hair

Epidermis

Nerve

Oil glands

Dermis

Sweat gland

Hair follicle

Fatty tissue

Blood vessels

sweat from your sweat glands. When this fluid dries, you feel even cooler.

Under the Skin

Skin's outer layer has dry, scaly, dead cells that are always being shed. Under that, living skin makes new cells. This layer has the pigment that colors the skin, and sunlight tans it even darker. The thick dermis layer under this has the sweat and oil glands, hair follicles, nerves, and blood vessels. Fat pads the skin below.

▲ Here is a cross-section drawing of human skin. The dead skin cells are on the top. Below them lies the living layer that makes new cells. The dermis under this is thicker. It contains nerves, hair follicles, sweat glands, oil glands, and blood vessels.

4: THE DIGESTIVE SYSTEM

The Mouth

The frenulum that connects your tongue to your mouth keeps you from choking on your tongue. ▶

Look in your open mouth in a mirror. Underneath your tongue is a membrane, called the frenulum, that keeps you from swallowing your tongue. You can also see the veins that take blood from the tongue. At the base of the frenulum is a tiny opening for one of the salivary glands. Saliva moistens food and makes swallowing easier.

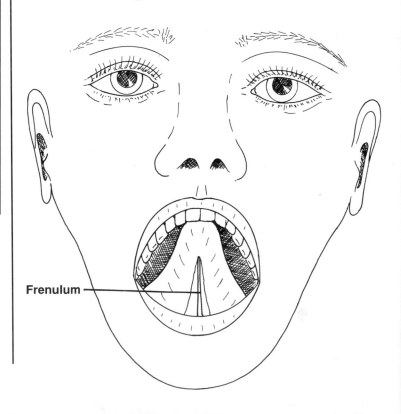

Frenulum

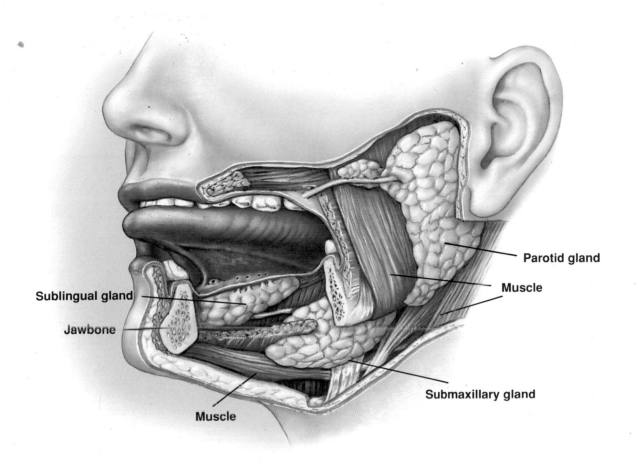

Parotid gland

Muscle

Sublingual gland

Jawbone

Submaxillary gland

Muscle

The roof of your mouth is the palate. Most of it is hard, but the back end is soft, and from it hangs a little tag called the uvula. Farther back lie the tonsils, tissue that collects microbes that can make you sick. Sometimes tonsils get infected and have to be taken out. The Eustachian tubes end in your throat. These tubes go up to the eardrum to keep the air pressure the same on both sides.

▲ The tongue has many muscles that move it for talking and eating. Larger muscles work your jaws. Your mouth has three pairs of salivary glands. Look under your tongue for the openings to these glands.

The Throat

The throat is where food, ▶ drink, and air must go through to the right places. The epiglottis is the valve that shuts off the windpipe so food doesn't get into it. The muscles that push food from your mouth to your stomach act without you having to think of using them.

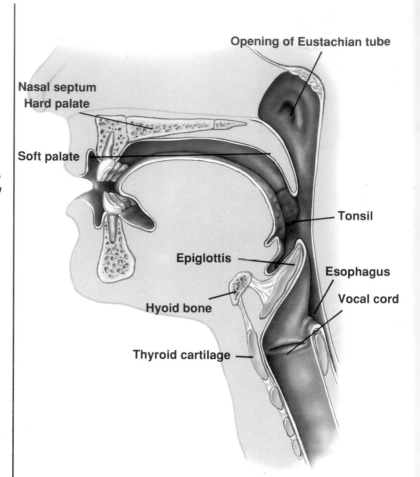

Nasal septum
Hard palate
Soft palate
Opening of Eustachian tube
Tonsil
Epiglottis
Esophagus
Vocal cord
Hyoid bone
Thyroid cartilage

Have you ever noticed that you can't swallow and breathe or talk at the same time? This is because your throat carefully controls its three jobs of talking, swallowing, and breathing.

Inside the Throat

The upper part of your throat is called the pharynx. Its muscles push food down into the throat. Over the top of the windpipe stands a valve — the epiglottis —

that keeps us from choking on food or swallowing air. The epiglottis acts like a trapdoor. When you swallow food, your nerves automatically shut the epiglottis over the windpipe, and the food slides past on its way to your stomach.

The upper part of your windpipe is the larynx, or voice box. It has two vocal cords, flaps of tissue that can be stretched like rubber bands to change the space between them. Air going out through this space vibrates the cords to make sounds. Your mouth and tongue shape the sounds into speech.

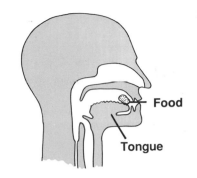

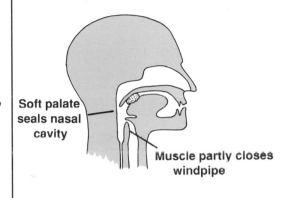

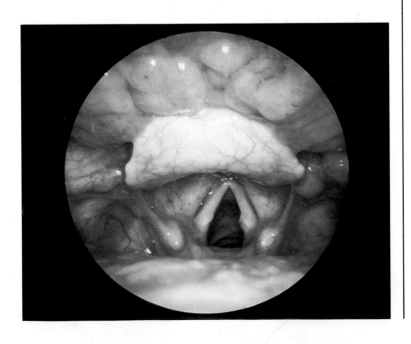

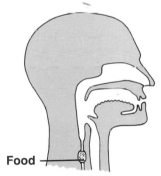

▲ When you swallow food, the soft palate rises to shut off the nose. The epiglottis also moves down to seal off the windpipe.

◀ The white flap is the epiglottis. Below it, the vocal cords make a V. Talking partly shuts the opening, and air breathed out vibrates the cords to make sounds — your voice.

The Stomach

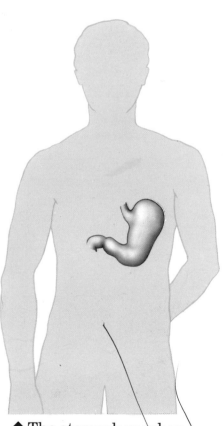

▲ The stomach reaches from behind the left ribs to behind the bellybutton.

The stomach is a muscular bag that passes food into the intestines. A ring of muscle at each end keeps the food inside. ▶

After you swallow food, it goes down the esophagus and into your stomach.

The Stomach in Action

The stomach makes a strong acid and several enzymes that break food down into tiny pieces. There are separate enzymes that digest proteins, sugars, starches, and fats. The acid also kills any microbes in the food. A slippery lining — the mucous membrane — protects the stomach from the acid. But if it can no longer protect the stomach, or if there is

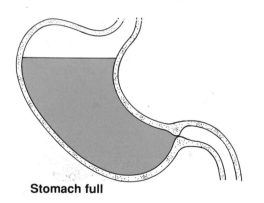

Stomach full

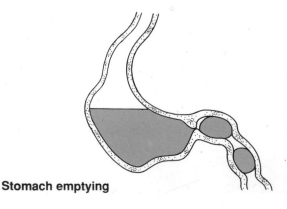

Stomach emptying

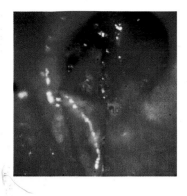
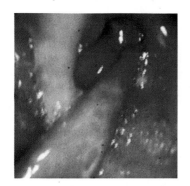
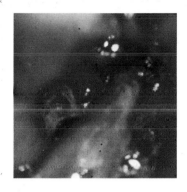
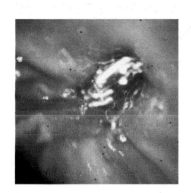

◀ These photographs show views of the inside of a living human stomach.

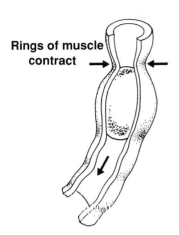

Rings of muscle contract →

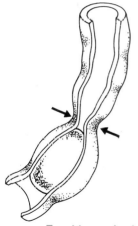

Food is pushed along

▲ These drawings show how muscle contractions pass along the intestines, mixing and pushing the food through. The stomach also mixes food this way.

What Does the Stomach Do?

• It feeds food slowly into the intestines.

• It makes gastric juices — the enzymes and acid that break up the food and kill microbes.

• It mixes the digestive juices with the food.

• It adds slippery mucin to help the food move.

too much acid, the stomach wall will burn, forming an ulcer. The muscles in the stomach's wall churn the food and slowly pass it into the intestines. Three to five hours after eating a meal, the stomach will be empty.

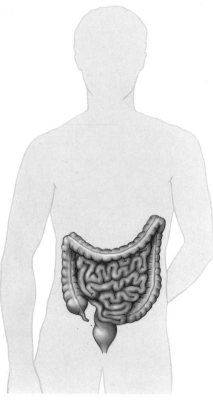

The Intestines

In your abdominal region, 28 feet (8.5 m) of tubelike intestines pass food from the stomach to the rectum. Most of this is the small intestine, which comes right after the stomach. The last four feet (1.5 m) form the large intestine.

Food for Life

When food enters the small intestine, bile and enzymes are added. Bile turns oils and fats into small drops so the fat enzyme can break them down into tiny nutrients. Other enzymes break down starch, sugar, and protein. When the nutrients are small enough, they can pass through the wall of the intestine. This wall is lined with

▲ Most of your intestines' 28 feet (8.5 m) form the small intestine, which digests food. The large intestine absorbs water and stores waste in the rectum.

Here is a close-up view of ▶ the villi inside the small intestine. Nutrients pass right into the blood vessels in the villi.

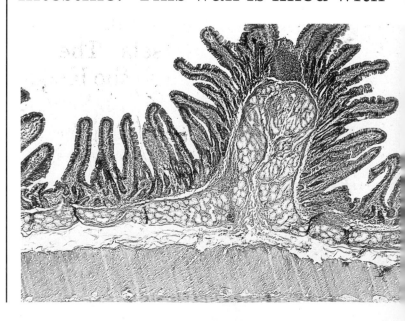

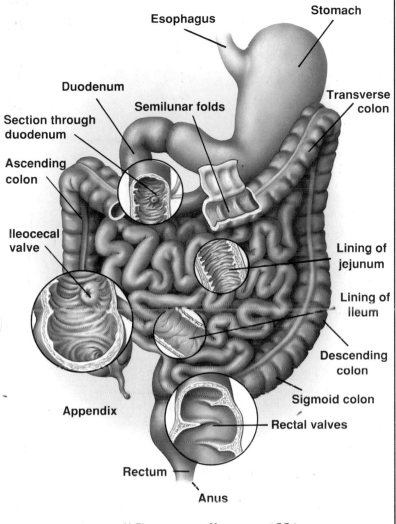

Esophagus

Stomach

Duodenum

Semilunar folds

Transverse colon

Section through duodenum

Ascending colon

Ileocecal valve

Lining of jejunum

Lining of ileum

Descending colon

Sigmoid colon

Rectal valves

Appendix

Rectum

Anus

◀ Each section of the intestines has a special lining to help it do a special job. The circles labeled with the sections' names show a close-up view of each lining. The large intestine is made up of the colon and the rectum. Rectal valves keep food wastes from backing up. The small intestine joins the colon at the ileocecal valve. In the close-up of the duodenum, you can see the opening where the bile and digestive enzymes enter.

very tiny "fingers" — villi — filled with blood vessels. The nutrients go right into the blood, which carries them to the liver. The liver builds them into the materials the body needs. Fibers and other wastes left over from your meal pass on into the large intestine. This takes out the water and stores the solid waste in the rectum until it leaves.

Facts and Feats

• Your intestines have enough surface area to clothe five people.

• It takes about 24 hours for a normal meal to pass from one end of your intestines to the other.

• People who eat only soft foods need a week to pass food all the way through their intestines.

• The intestines form a gas that sometimes explodes when a surgeon opens up the intestines.

Waste Matter

This is a cross-section ▶ view of a human kidney. The cortex contains the nephrons — tiny tubes that take wastes from the blood to make urine.

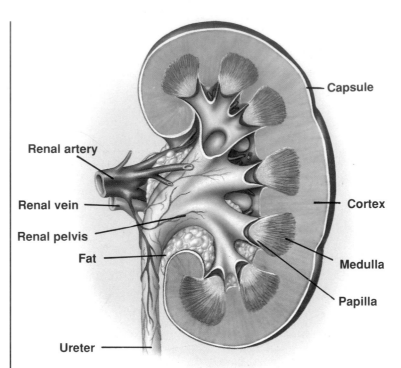

Capsule

Renal artery

Renal vein

Renal pelvis

Fat

Cortex

Medulla

Papilla

Ureter

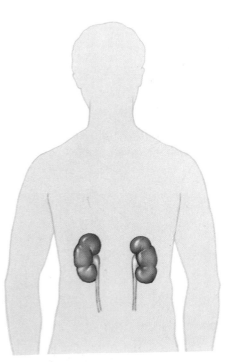

▲ The kidneys are in the middle of your back. The right kidney is a little lower than the left one.

Many bacteria live inside the intestines. These bacteria make up half the weight of the feces that form. The rest is made up of fibers and other food wastes. All this is stored in the rectum. But the wastes from the body's cells go into the blood, which carries them to the kidneys.

The Kidneys

Each kidney has over a million tiny structures, called nephrons, that take water out of the blood. They put back the exact amount of water the body needs to work right. They also put back the useful things, such as nutrients

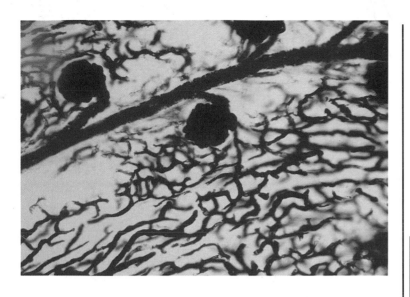

This picture shows a kidney with the blood vessels stained red. The dark spots are knots of vessels where the wastes are removed. The nephrons that collect the waste are not stained, so you cannot see them in this picture.

from food. The unwanted things, like excess salt, stay behind in the nephron tubes with the excess water to make urine. The urine runs through tubes to the bladder, which stores it until it is emptied. Every day about 45 gallons (170 liters) of fluid go through the kidneys. Almost all of this is water that the kidneys return to the blood.

Did You Know?

• Infections or other diseases can make stones form in the kidneys. These stones can hurt, and they may keep urine from leaving the body. This can cause illness.

• Surgeons used to cut open the body to take out the stones. Now they can put a tiny loop right through a person's back into the kidney and pull the stones out. But the best way is to break up the kidney stones with sound waves. Then the urine washes out the tiny pieces.

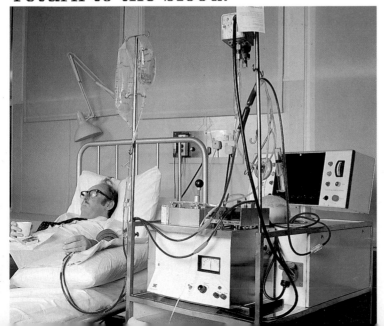

When people's kidneys do not work right, they must use a kidney machine to clean their blood. Just think — one tiny kidney does the job of this big machine!

5: | GLANDS

The Thymus

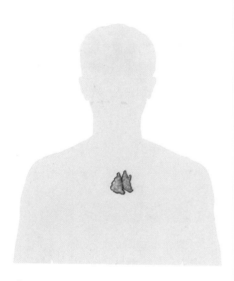

▲ This drawing shows the location of the thymus. The thymus turns white blood cells into T cells that can fight infection.

The thymus lies behind your breastbone. This gland is filled with white blood cells that keep you from getting sick. Most of them are in the cortex — the outer part of the thymus lobes.

Disease Protection

The thymus makes antibodies. These are chemicals that destroy microbes that can cause disease. The thymus also makes T cells. T cells start out as white blood cells made in the bone marrow that go to the thymus, where they multiply. The thymus then

Did You Know?

• Rats fed thymus extract had larger, faster-growing babies.

• Birds that do not have a thymus lay eggs that have soft shells.

More about the Thymus

• Children born without a thymus can die from infections that do not bother people with one. One boy lived for 10 years in a plastic bubble to protect him from infection.

• Adults who lose their thymus by surgery still keep the protection against disease that they developed when younger.

• When animals become exhausted, their thymus wastes away to nearly nothing.

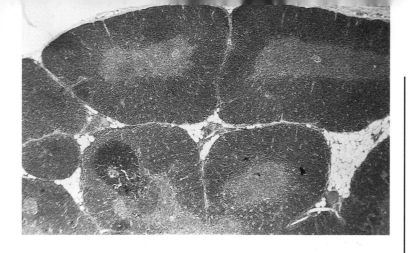

◀ This microscopic section of the thymus has been stained to show the lobes. The dark purple around each lobe is the cortex, which is mostly white blood cells. The pale center has fewer white cells.

This drawing shows that the thymus is biggest in young people. The older you grow, the smaller your thymus becomes. Old people have almost no ◀ thymus left.

changes them into T cells — the T is for thymus. These cells can now fight against many different infections — bacterial, virus, and fungus. The thymus also helps fight against cancer cells.

One interesting experiment showed that tadpoles grew faster if they were fed part of a thymus. ▼

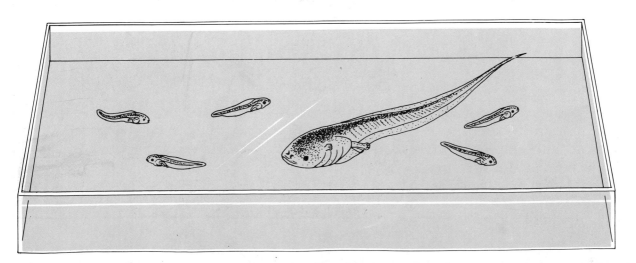

The Pineal and the Pituitary

Here is the pineal gland, ▶ tucked deep inside the brain. It is only the size of a pea.

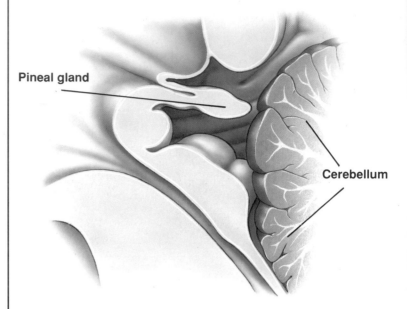

Pineal gland

Cerebellum

Deep inside your brain are two small glands called the pineal gland and the pituitary gland. In some animals the pineal gland acts as an extra eye. The pineal gland seems to help humans detect light. This may explain why we feel gloomy on cloudy days and more cheerful when the Sun is shining.

The Pituitary Gland

This gland produces many chemicals, called hormones, that act on other parts of the body. They control the thyroid and adrenal glands, the reproductive organs, and the rate of growth.

Did You Know?

• In some fish the pineal gland works as an third eye. The lamprey eel's third eye even has a lens. This eye detects light so the lamprey can make itself darker at night or lighter in the day. This helps keep its enemies from seeing it. Other fish and lizards may also have this extra eye.

• People who live where winters are dark and long, such as Alaska, can sit in front of bright lights to keep themselves from becoming gloomy.

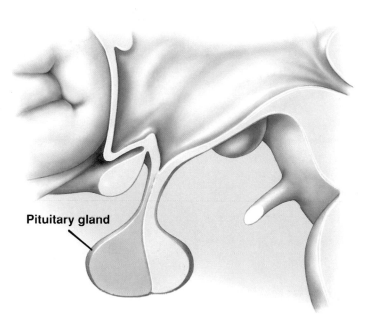

Pituitary gland

◀ The pituitary gland is also located deep inside the brain. Sometimes it is called the "master gland" of the body because it controls other glands.

Sandy Allen is much bigger than she should be because her pituitary gland made too much growth hormone. ▼

Too much growth hormone makes a person grow much bigger than normal. Too little growth hormone keeps the body from reaching its normal size. But this happens very rarely. Children grow at different rates, and short children almost always catch up.

Pineal eye

Lamprey

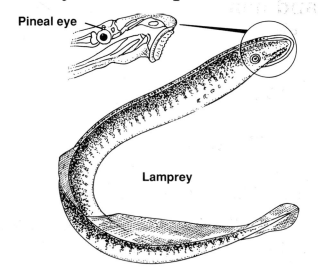

◀ The pineal gland of the lamprey eel has grown into a third eye, complete with lens and retina.

41

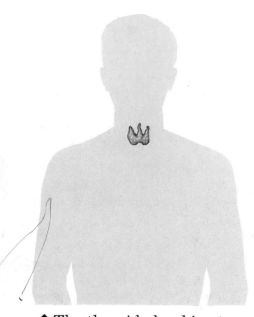

The Thyroid

The thyroid gland grows as two lobes at the base of the neck. This gland controls how fast or slow the body uses energy. If your thyroid speeded up the use of energy, it could become larger — this is called a goiter. Then you would be overactive. If your thyroid slowed down, you would become tired and worn out. These diseases can be treated with medicine. The thyroid also needs iodine to stay healthy.

The Parathyroid Glands

At the back of your thyroid are four little glands like small peas,

▲ The thyroid gland is at the base of the neck, partly wrapped around the windpipe, just under the voice box.

Here is a front view (top) ▶ and back view (bottom) of the thyroid and parathyroid glands.

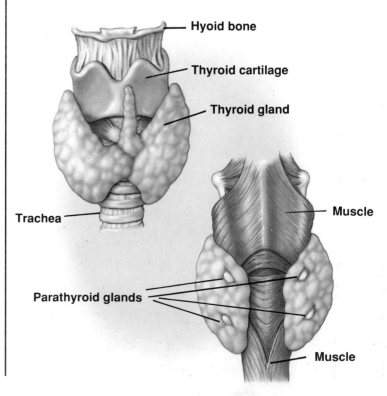

Hyoid bone

Thyroid cartilage

Thyroid gland

Trachea

Muscle

Parathyroid glands

Muscle

42

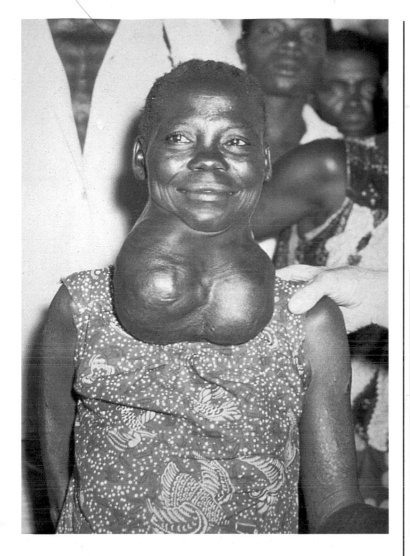

People in many parts of the world get goiters — large thyroids — because their diets do not have enough iodine. Often, there are not enough doctors in developing nations to help these people. The goiters can keep on growing for years.

Did You Know?

If the thyroid doesn't get enough iodine from food, it will grow too large — this is called a goiter. In the United States, goiter was once common in the "goiter belt" — the Great Lakes region and central mountain areas. Using iodized salt regularly now prevents this disease.

called parathyroid glands. They help keep enough calcium in your body so that your bones stay strong. People with overactive parathyroids become depressed and their bones get soft. Without parathyroids, your muscles will go into severe contractions, or convulsions, that can result in death. This condition can be treated by hormones.

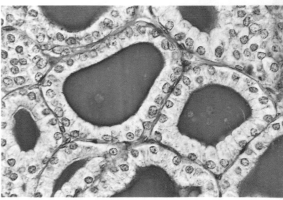

This is a photograph of a thyroid gland that has been stained. The large spaces that are colored purple store the thyroid's hormone.

43

The Pancreas

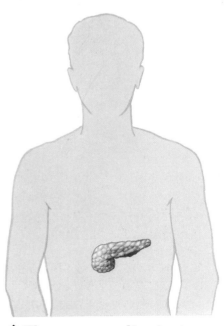

▲ The pancreas lies just behind the stomach.

The pancreas has two kinds of tissues. One kind of tissue makes enzymes that digest your food. The other kind of tissue helps your body cells use sugar for energy. When food leaves your stomach, it enters the first 12 inches (30 cm) of your small intestine — the duodenum. This entry signals the pancreas to pour pancreatic juice into the duodenum. The pancreatic juice is a mixture of different kinds of enzymes, each one digesting — or breaking down — one kind of food so that its nutrients are small enough to pass right into the blood vessels in the walls of the small intestine. Bile also enters the duodenum to help the enzymes digest fats and oils.

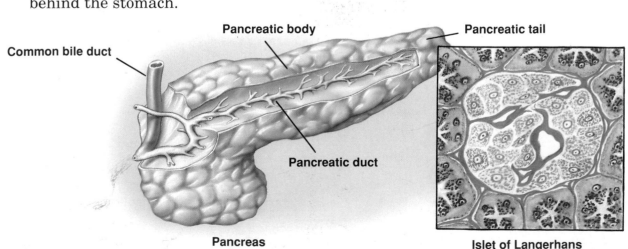

Common bile duct

Pancreatic body

Pancreatic tail

Pancreatic duct

Pancreas

Islet of Langerhans

Diabetes

The islets of Langerhans are tissue islands in the pancreas. They make insulin, a hormone that moves sugar from the blood to the body's cells, which use it for energy. People without enough insulin have diabetes, a disease with high blood sugar levels that causes illness and death. Most diabetics must take insulin to stay healthy.

Adrenal Glands — Fight or Flight

On the top of each kidney sits a small adrenal gland. The adrenals help keep the minerals and water of your body in balance. These glands also help you face danger. When something threatens you, the adrenals pour out hormones that prepare your body to fight the threat, or run away from it. This is called the "fight or flight" response. One of these hormones is called adrenaline. When these emergency hormones enter your blood, you stop digesting food for the time being. Your heart starts pumping faster and harder. More blood flows to your muscles. Extra sugar for more energy enters your bloodstream. You are now ready to fight the danger, or run away from it.

◀ This boy has diabetes. Every day he must give himself a shot of insulin, because his body does not make it. If he did not do this, he could go into a coma and die. Some diabetics can control their sugar level with a strict diet. Others can take medicine by mouth.

6: MOVEMENT

Muscles

▲ Under a microscope, muscles have bands, or striations. These bands are where the muscle fibers slide closer together when the muscle bunches up, or contracts. The striated muscles are also called voluntary muscles.

Muscle makes your body move. It also keeps your body still. You can stand still only because your muscles are holding you upright. The largest muscles are the gluteus muscles — the ones you sit on. The smallest muscles are the eye muscles.

How Muscles Work

The nerves send signals that make the muscles move. Muscles cannot push; they only pull. So when you stick out your tongue, the muscles pull across the tongue and force it out. Your arm or leg moves when a big muscle on one side pulls on the bones. A muscle is attached to a bone by a tendon — a strip of tough, stretchable tissue. The big arm and leg muscles are voluntary. This means you can decide to use them. Under a microscope, you can see bands, or striations, in this kind of muscle. These bands are where the muscle fibers move closer together when the muscle contracts, or bunches up.

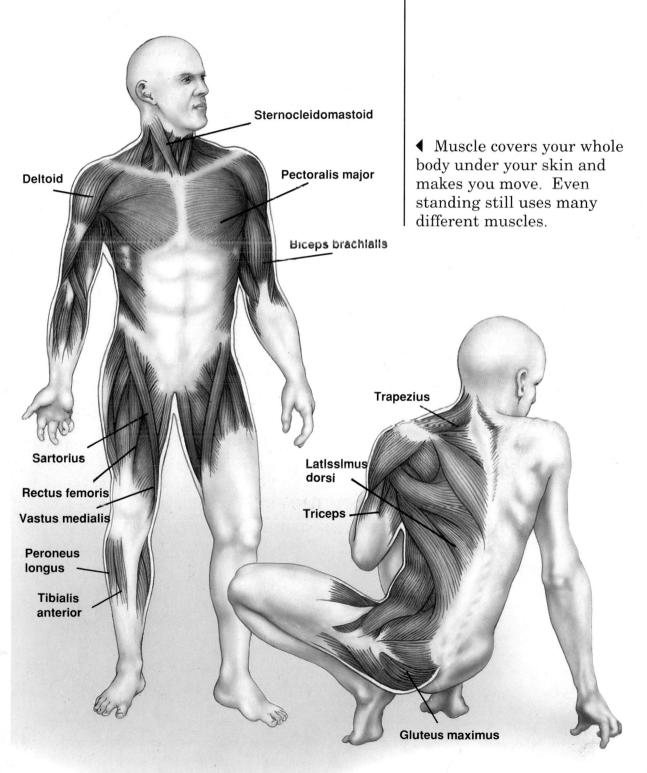

Sternocleidomastoid

Deltoid

Pectoralis major

◀ Muscle covers your whole body under your skin and makes you move. Even standing still uses many different muscles.

Biceps brachialis

Sartorius

Rectus femoris

Vastus medialis

Peroneus longus

Tibialis anterior

Trapezius

Latissimus dorsi

Triceps

Gluteus maximus

Reflexes

Cross one leg over the other, then tap lightly just below the kneecap. Your leg will jerk up. You cannot stop this reflex action. ▼

A reflex is any quick action your body makes that is the same each time and that you don't think about. Reflexes protect the body from harm. Something must stimulate — or set off — the reflex. If you burn yourself, a reflex jerks your hand away. Reflexes use both striated muscle and smooth muscle.

Smooth Muscles

Many muscles in your body do not have striations. They are smooth muscles, and they are built for steady, automatic movements. They are not attached to bones, and they keep working, day after day, without you thinking about them. Smooth muscle in your

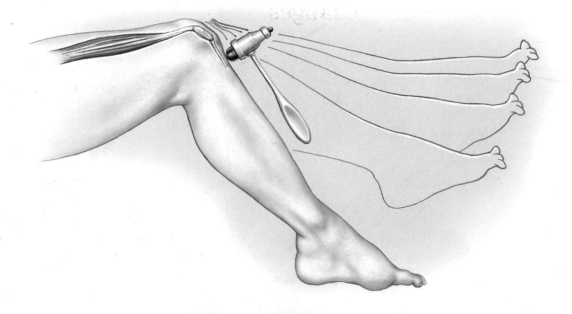

stomach and intestines keeps your food steadily churning. Smooth muscle in the blood vessels lets more or less blood through if you get hot or cold. Smooth muscle makes the pupils of your eyes get bigger or smaller as the light changes.

▲ Smooth muscles work without you thinking about them. If you are surprised or frightened, you will feel hair stand up on the back of your neck. The hair on this coyote's back is standing on end. This reflex makes it look bigger to its enemies.

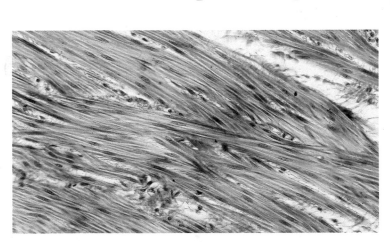

◀ This section from inside the abdomen shows smooth muscle fibers. The body cells are stained green and the smooth muscle looks gray. Smooth muscles work automatically. For example, they make the pupil of your eye get larger or smaller as the light changes.

The Heart

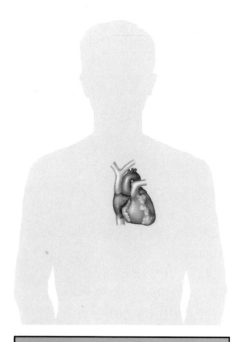

The heart is a pump with four rooms, or chambers, inside. Heart muscle — cardiac muscle — has some striations, but it is not under conscious control. A heartbeat comes from the opening and closing of the heart valves as they steer the blood through the different chambers.

How the Heart Works

The heart lies between the lungs and a little more on the left side. The heart has two sides, each

About the Heart

• Mammals and birds have hearts with four chambers. Frog hearts have three, and fish hearts have only two!

• If a heart attack stops blood taking oxygen to the brain, death or brain injury can result.

• Anger and excitement make the heart beat faster than normal. So does eating.

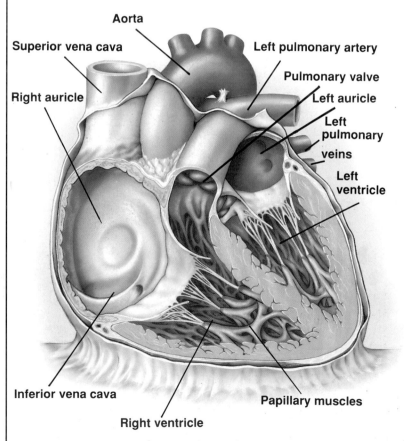

Aorta

Superior vena cava

Left pulmonary artery

Right auricle

Pulmonary valve

Left auricle

Left pulmonary veins

Left ventricle

Inferior vena cava

Papillary muscles

Right ventricle

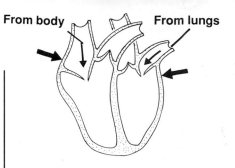

From body   From lungs

with a small chamber — the auricle — on top and a large chamber — the ventricle — below. All the chambers have valves that control the blood flow. Blood low in oxygen collects in the right auricle. It goes into the right ventricle, where strong muscles pump it through an artery to the lungs. There the blood gets fresh oxygen and returns to the left auricle. It enters the left ventricle, which sends it through the aorta to flow around the entire body and come back to the heart.

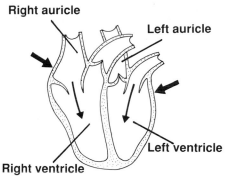

Right auricle   Left auricle

Left ventricle

Right ventricle

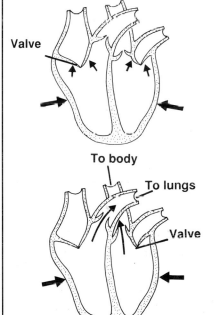

Valve

To body   To lungs

Valve

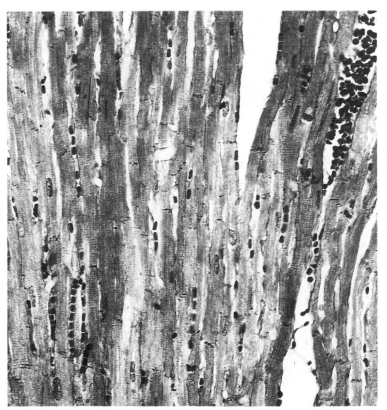

▲ The left sides of these pictures, from the top down, show how blood enters the heart and goes to the lungs. The right sides show how blood goes out into the body.

◀ Heart muscle is like both striated and smooth muscle.

7: ON THE SURFACE

Hair

These are human hairs as ▶ seen by electron microscope. You can see the scaly surface of the hairs. The scales are made of protein, and their shape is different from one person to another.

▲ This man has let the hair on his face grow to produce a beard.

Each hair grows from a small pouch in your skin, called a follicle. You have about 10,000 follicles on your head. The base, or root, of the hair is like a bulb, and it grows new hair.

How Hair Grows
A hair follicle grows hair for several years, then stops. The

old hair drops out while the follicle rests for several months. Then it starts growing hair again. Melanin is the pigment that colors most hair. Red hair is from another pigment. As people age, the color leaves their hair and it looks gray because it is hollow. When old hair follicles stop growing hair faster than

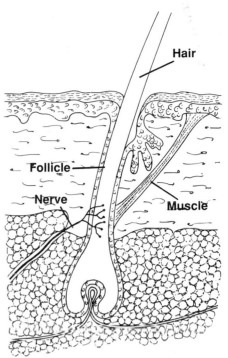

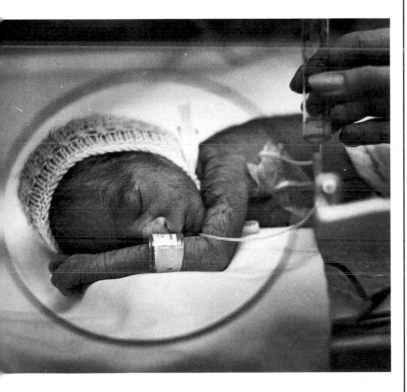

Did You Know?

Hair not only helps keep you warm, it also tells you that something is near you. A light touch on a hair is picked up by nerve endings around hair roots (shown above).

new ones can start growing it, the person — almost always a man — becomes bald. Straight follicles grow straight hair, and curved follicles grow hair that is wavy or curly.

◀ Before babies are born, they are covered with fine, downy hair called lanugo. This soon goes away, to be replaced by body hair. Real head hair grows much later. This tiny baby, born six weeks early, is still covered with lanugo.

Nails

This drawing shows the ▶ inside of your fingertip. The nail matrix is under the root of the nail (top). You can see the pink skin through the nail. The cross-section (bottom) shows how the nail protects the bone at the tips of our fingers.

▲ Horse hoofs grow from the horse's middle toe. These "nails" are very thick and strong. In fact, nailing on horseshoes does not hurt the horse.

Nails are made from a protein called keratin. This protein also makes up hair, hoofs, feathers, horns, claws, and turtle shells. Nails protect the ends of fingers and toes. Many animals use claws as weapons, or for digging. A man in India stopped cutting

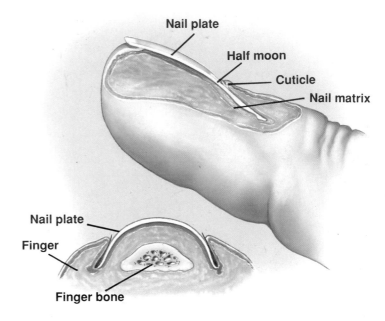

his nails in 1952. His fingernails grew to an average of over 21 inches (55 cm)! His left thumb-nail was 27.5 inches (70 cm) long.

How Nails Grow
The nail you see is the nail plate. The part going into the skin is the root. Under the root lies the nail

matrix, the tissue that grows the nail cells. The new cells keep pushing the old dead cells out of the skin, where they harden in the air. Air pockets form half-moons. Here is where the nail will loosen if it gets injured. A new nail will start to grow under the old one. Smaller injuries only make white marks on the nail.

▲ Human nails can grow to amazing lengths — up to 25 inches (64 cm) long! But they usually break off naturally.

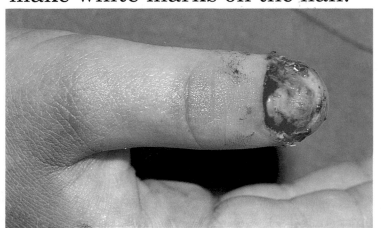

◀ This child lost a nail in an accident. A new nail will grow back in about two months.

Teeth

There are 20 primary teeth (left) and 32 adult teeth ▶ (right). The adult third molars — wisdom teeth — often become impacted, or stuck between the other teeth and the jawbone. Then they have to be taken out.

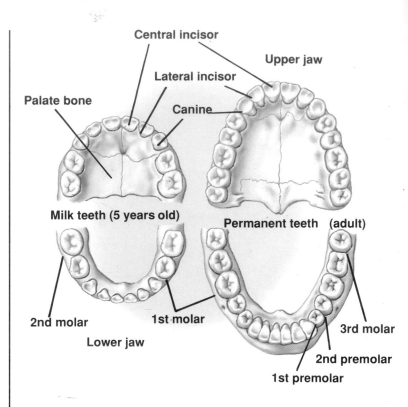

Central incisor

Upper jaw

Lateral incisor

Palate bone

Canine

Milk teeth (5 years old)

Permanent teeth   (adult)

2nd molar

1st molar

3rd molar

Lower jaw

2nd premolar

1st premolar

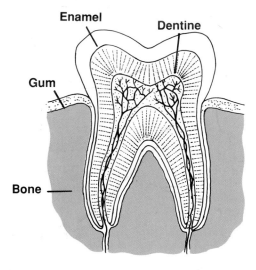

Enamel

Dentine

Gum

Bone

▲ This drawing of the inside of a human tooth shows a hard layer of enamel on its crown — the part above the gum. The tooth's center has blood vessels and nerves. If this part gets infected, it can make the tooth ache.

Humans have two sets of teeth. The first are the 20 primary, or milk, teeth. They start to come in when a baby is about seven months old. At around six years of age, you begin getting your adult, or permanent, teeth. Almost all of the second set of 32 permanent teeth are in place by around 13 years of age.

Types of Teeth

Adult teeth are made up mostly of a hard material called dentine. Inside this is pulp — soft tissue that has blood vessels and nerves. Enamel covers the tooth

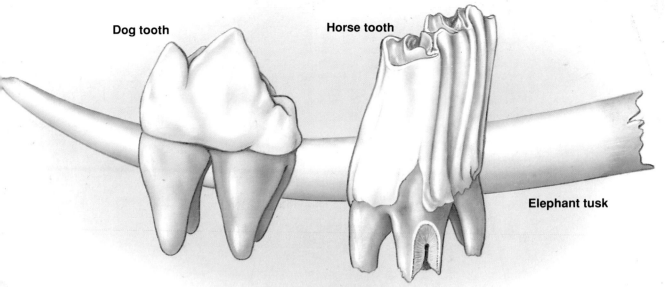

Dog tooth

Horse tooth

Elephant tusk

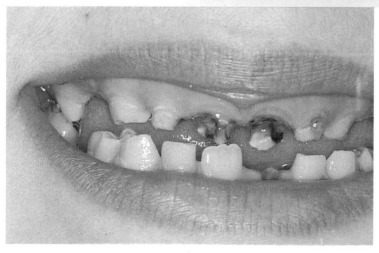

▲ Meat-eaters' teeth are sharp, and plant-eaters' teeth are flat. Elephant tusks are special teeth used for digging.

◀ People who eat too much sugar and starch can have very bad tooth decay.

outside the gum. This is the hardest structure in the body. But enamel will not grow back if decay breaks through. The roots of adult teeth are cemented into sockets in the jawbone. Incisors at the front of the mouth are for cutting. Next to them are the canines, which can tear meat. The large molars and premolars at the back are for grinding.

When Milk Teeth Arrive

Name of tooth	Average time it comes in
Lower central incisors	7.5 months
Upper central incisors	9.5 months
Upper premolars	15.5 months
Lower premolars	16 months
Upper and lower canines	21 months
Second premolars	26.5 months

8: THE NEXT GENERATION

Babies

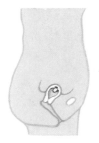 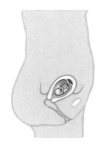 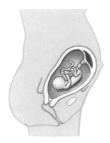 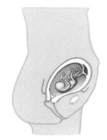 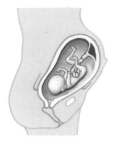

7 weeks   **3 months**   **4 months**   **5 months**   **6 months**

 A baby grows quickly. As time goes by, it changes from a clump of cells into a human being. The growing baby gets food and oxygen from its mother's blood.

The egg cell of a human being can just barely be seen by the naked eye. It starts to develop in the mother's body when it is joined by a sperm cell from the father.

The Developing Child

The fertilized egg cell quickly divides into many cells. By five weeks the baby is only a quarter of an inch (6-7 mm) long. Already it has eyes and a heart, which beats rapidly. The baby grows inside a sack filled with fluid to protect it from bumps. An umbilical cord connects the growing baby to the placenta — a disk-shaped organ that develops soon after the baby begins to

Facts and Feats

Babies are usually born headfirst. A few babies come out feet first. Once in a while, a baby lies right across the birth canal. Then a doctor may have to operate by cutting open the womb and lifting the baby out. We call this a Caesarean operation. A butcher did the first Caesarean, on his wife in 1500. She and the baby both lived.

form. The placenta is attached inside the mother's womb, and it passes food and oxygen to the baby's blood from the mother. Some drugs can also get through

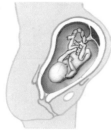
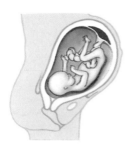
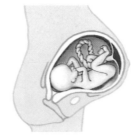
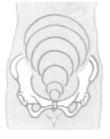

7 months   8 months   9 months (ready for birth)   Frontal view of uterus

and harm the baby. The baby's wastes go through the placenta and into the mother's blood.

Birth

After nine months, the baby is ready to be born. Muscles start squeezing the mother's womb harder and harder, and the birth canal gets bigger. At last, the baby is pushed out into the world.

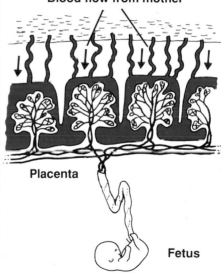

Blood flow from mother

Placenta

Fetus

▲ The mother's and the baby's blood do not mix. Food and wastes go through the placenta. Some drugs can get through the placenta and harm the unborn baby.

◀ At the end of nine months, a new baby is born.

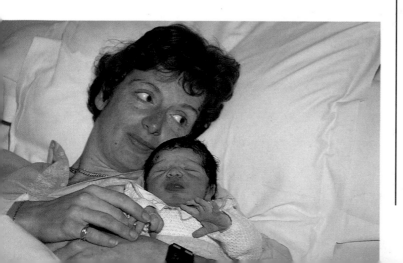

59

Glossary

Axon: The longest branch of a nerve cell. It carries nerve impulses away from the body of the cell.

Cell: The smallest living unit. Cells are the basic living units from which all living organisms and their parts are made.

Cerebellum: The part of the brain near the back of the skull. It controls the coordination of smooth muscle and voluntary muscle.

Cerebral cortex: The thin, highly folded outer layer of the cerebral halves, or hemispheres, which are the largest parts of the brain. This is where thinking takes place.

Cervical: Of or belonging to the neck.

Conscious: Aware of something; knowing something within oneself. (See also **Unconscious**.)

Convulsions: Sudden, violent, and often painful contractions of a muscle or muscles.

Cortex: The outermost part or layer of any gland, organ, or other body structure.

Environment: The surroundings in which something lives. The environment is made up of everything that can affect the growth and behavior of a living thing, including plants, animals, and other life forms.

Enzymes: Chemicals that speed up the natural change of one substance into another in the body while staying unchanged themselves. Enzymes are proteins made by living organisms.

Gastric: Of or belonging to the stomach. For example, gastric juice is a fluid mixture that is made by the stomach.

Gill slits: The openings on the head of a fish that let the water leave its body after it flows over the gills, which take out the oxygen the fish needs. In its mother's womb, a human baby goes through an early stage where it has slits in its neck that resemble a fish's gill slits. These close up as it continues to grow and develop in the womb.

Gland: An organ of the body that makes chemical substances, mostly for use by the body. The thyroid gland, the thymus, and the sweat glands are examples.

Hormones: Chemical messengers released in tiny amounts into the bloodstream by certain glands and carried by the blood to produce effects in other parts of the body.

Lobe: A rounded section or part of a structure, such as the lobe of the ear. Many structures of the body are divided into lobes, such as the lung, brain, glands, and other parts.

Lumbar: Of or belonging to the back and sides between the bottom of the ribs and the pelvis in a human or other mammal.

Marrow: A soft, fatty substance that is found inside bones. The bone marrow makes both red and white blood cells.

Medulla: The inside part of a gland, organ, or other structure that has a cortex.

Membrane: A thin, flexible, sheetlike tissue that connects different organs or that lines an organ or other part of the body.

Microbes: Very small living things visible under a microscope, especially the bacteria, protists, or fungi that can cause diseases.

Mucin: The slippery material in saliva, mucous membrane, and other tissues and fluids of the body. Mucin mixes with food in the stomach to help it move smoothly through the intestines.

Nucleus: The small mass in most plant and animal cells that carries a cell's inherited traits and directs the activities the cell needs to live, such as growth and reproduction.

Nutrients: The parts of foods that the body uses, especially when they are broken down into particles small enough to pass into the blood.

Organ: A recognizable form made up by a group of tissues which work together to do a particular job for the body. For example, the liver, the eye, and the intestines are organs.

Ossicle: A small bone. The ossicles in the ear are the smallest bones of the human body.

Pigment: The natural coloring of a tissue. Pigments can occur in any organ or other part of a plant or animal.

Pitch: The quality of a sound that tells you how high or low it is.

Placenta: A flat, spongy, circular, blood-rich organ to which a developing baby is attached by the umbilical cord while in the mother's womb. Food and oxygen for the growing baby travels through the placenta, which keeps most harmful substances from reaching the baby. But some drugs can still travel through the placenta and damage the baby. (See also **Umbilical cord**.)

Platelets: Very small pieces of cells in the blood that quickly make a temporary plug in any break that occurs in the tissues or blood vessels. This stops the bleeding until a normal blood clot can form and replace it. Large cells in the bone marrow, called megakaryocytes, break into small pieces to produce platelets.

Proteins: A group of complex chemical compounds that are basic building blocks of all living things and which take part in many of the ways that they work.

Reflex: A fast, unconscious action taken by a set of muscles because of some stimulation. The signals that put the muscles into action come from a special nerve circuit, called a reflex arc, which travels through the spinal cord. The nerve signals do not go through the brain because the reflex acts faster than you can think and decide what to do.

Retina: A tissue that lines the inside of the eye. It is made up of several layers of nerve cells, and one layer of special cells — the rods and the cones. The rods see dim light best. They are used in black-and-white vision and for detecting motion. The cones detect color, and see bright images best. A small dip in the center of the retina, the fovea, has cones but no rods. This is where your sight is the sharpest. Nerve fibers from the retina come together to form the optic nerve, which carries the image signals to the brain. The place where the optic nerve leaves the retina cannot see. We call this place the blind spot.

Sacral: Of or belonging to the sacrum, a bone near the base of the spine that is part of the pelvis.

Sinuses: The name given to hollows, or spaces, in different organs or parts of the body. For example, there are sinuses in the bones of the face.

Suture: The line made when two bones grow together to make a firm seam, or joint, that does not move.

Synapse: The microscopic gap between branches of two neighboring nerve cells. Chemicals called neurotransmitters carry messages across this gap from one cell to another.

Taste buds: Microscopic clusters of cells, each cluster buried in the surface of the tongue behind a tiny opening. Nerve fibers connect each taste bud to the brain. Different taste buds can detect sweet, sour, salt, and bitter. The tongue has most of the body's taste buds, but there are also some scattered around inside the entire mouth and part of the throat.

Tendon: A band of tough, nonstretching tissue that attaches a muscle to a bone.

Thoracic: Of or belonging to the thorax, or chest. The thorax is the part of the body between the neck and the abdomen.

Tissue: A group of cells that are much alike, doing the same job. Different kinds of tissue make up structures like an organ, gland, or other part of the body.

Toxin: A poison produced by a living organism. Toxins can cause illness. Some microbes that cause disease make toxins.

Ulcer: A small pit or crater made in the lining of the stomach or the duodenum by the stomach's acid. An ulcer can result if the membrane no longer protects the wall of the stomach or duodenum from the acid, or if there is too much stomach acid in these areas. Ulcers are often painful and need to be treated.

Umbilical cord: A tough cord of tissue that connects a developing baby at its navel, or bellybutton, with the placenta inside the mother's womb. Food, oxygen, and the baby's wastes travel through the umbilical cord between the baby and the placenta. (See also **Placenta**.)

Valve: One or more flaps in an organ or passageway of the body. Valves control the flow of fluids by closing like a trapdoor to prevent the fluid from going in the opposite direction.

Vertebra (*plural*: **vertebrae**): One of the bones of the spine. Vertebrae are linked by flexible joints. They protect the spinal cord, which runs through their centers.

Viruses: A group of extremely tiny living things, many of which cause disease. Viruses can reproduce only inside the cells of a living plant, animal, or other life form. Viruses might be the smallest living things.

Vitamins: A group of chemical compounds that the body needs to function properly. Lack of vitamins in the diet can lead to disease. For example, lack of vitamin C results in the disease of scurvy, a disease that sailors in former years sometimes used to get on long voyages, when they did not have fresh food, which contains vitamin C, to eat.

Womb: The part of a woman's body that holds and protects the developing baby during pregnancy. It is also called the uterus.

Index

A **boldface** number shows that the entry is illustrated on that page. The same page often has text about the entry, too.